SCAMPER

SCAMPER

Creative Games and Activities for Imagination Development

Bob Eberle

Routledge
Taylor & Francis Group

NEW YORK AND LONDON

First published in 2008 by Prufrock Press Inc.

Published in 2021 by Routledge
605 Third Avenue, New York, NY 10017
2 Park Square, Milton Park, Abingdon, Oxon OX14 4RN

Routledge is an imprint of the Taylor & Francis Group, an informa business

ISBN: 9781593633462 (pbk)

Contents

Acknowledgements

The SCAMPER games have been tested with children as young as 3 years old up to college students and veteran teachers in-service. As a result of testing, it has been possible to receive valuable information pertinent to the publication of this work. I am indeed grateful to the many friends who responded and whom I now acknowledge:

Connie Bagley, Catherine Bain, Leah Biessman, J. C. Blair, Carol Brueggeman, Rex S. Gourley, Carol M. Greenwood, Connie Ham, Velma M. Hogge, Donna Kelly, Marion S. Masica, DeAnne T. McConnell, Virginia Merrill, Judy Miller, E. V. Millet, Karen Strand, Nancy Suhre, Beverly Varty, Dorothy Werblo, Margaret Wheaton, Gene G. Wilson, and Margaret Woods.

And a very special acknowledgement to those who made editorial suggestions and contributions for the improvement of the work:

Karen Agne, Berenice Bleedorn, Jeanne Brunworth, Starr Cline, Jo Doersam, Carol Downing, Pat Doyle, Gretchen Duling, George Frack, Ruthanna D. Frack, Kathy Gerber, Jodie Grinter, Helen C. Hamman, Jean Helm, Jennine Jackson, Dorothy M. Jones, Bobbie Kraver, Linette Maedge, DeAnne McConnel, Phyllis McDonald, Helen C. Mitchell, Ruth B. Noller, Sidney J. Parnes, Bev Schaake, Robert Stanish, Nancy Suhre, Pansy Torrance, Shirley Ward, Frank E. Williams, and Carol Wittig.

The author also wishes to acknowledge his debt to Richard de Mille whose book, *Put Your Mother on the Ceiling* (1967), served as a model for the cueing technique used in SCAMPER.

Introduction

What's in the Word SCAMPER?

SCAMPER: To run playfully about, as a child . . .
When you stop to think about this definition, there is really nothing much wrong with scampering. In fact, it might be a good thing to do, especially if you are looking for imaginative ideas. Everybody can have ideas, lots of ideas—sometimes, good ideas. Running playfully about in the world of make-believe is a visionary activity that helps to produce ideas. Of course, there are ways to go about scampering that will make an individual a better player. And that, of course, is exactly what we hope to do.

The purpose of this book is to assist children to maintain and, hopefully, to improve their imaginative ability. In some cases, adults may also benefit. SCAMPER games provide an opportunity to learn and practice idea-getting techniques that are the craft of authors, inventors, and composers. These same techniques have been successfully put to work in business and industry to create new products, improve methods of operation, and solve a variety of problems.

Imagination is an act of forming mental images, pictures of what is not actually present to the senses. It is the ability to see the unseen. Creative imagination is the ability to form unique and original mental images.

The process of creative imagination is one of rearranging or manipulating information that is drawn from the memory store. Knowledge recalled is subject to adaptation, combination, or other intellectual operations that serve to produce creative ideas. Checklisting techniques are of great value in the production of creative ideas. In brief, a checklist contains questions or suggestions that prompt and stimulate an individual to form creative ideas. The SCAMPER techniques draw heavily from the famous Idea Spurring Checklist developed by Alex Osborn.

In playing the SCAMPER games, individuals are cued to think imaginatively through the application of the checklisting techniques, which are incorporated into the games. In doing so, players are guided into fanciful and imaginative thought. Elegant, fantastic, and unrestrained visualization is brought about when creative thinking processes are applied to familiar objects or situations. Existing knowledge and experience provides the material to be manipulated in the quest for new and original images.

The word SCAMPER serves to describe the mental activity the games are intended to bring about. Each of the seven letters is also the initial letter of the word phrases that make up the checklist used to create the SCAMPER games. These word phrases, along with accompanying questions, are formed on the following page.

For further instruction on how to extend and create your own SCAMPER lessons, consult Appendix A: SCAMPER on Your Own (p. 74). As well, you can learn how to modify SCAMPER games for use as icebreaking and brainstorming activities with adults in Appendix B: SCAMPER With Adults (p. 76). For more information on the thinking and feeling processes associated with creative expression, see Appendix C: Creative Imagination Development, and the accompanying model in Appendix D (pp. 80–83). Finally, further reading to enhance your understanding of the theory behind the SCAMPER games can be found in Resources for Imagery and Creativity (pp. 85–86).

SCAMPERing With the Experts

For years, educators and psychologists have expressed an increasing interest in the perceptive, imaginative, and creative abilities of children. Frequently, these talents are overlooked in the schools. It is necessary for imaginative and creative talent to be cultivated and rewarded if a child is to develop into a healthy, mentally alert, productive adult.

Too often, adults seem dedicated to the task of rushing children into the real world as quickly as possible. The pressures to conform that are placed on children by adults are considered to be a major cause for

SCAMPER Checklist

S **Substitute** — To have a person or thing act or serve in the place of another. Who else? What else? Other place? Time?

C **Combine** — To bring together, to unite. Combine what? Bring whom together? Combine purposes? Ideas? Materials?

A **Adjust** — To adapt for the purpose of suiting a condition. Reshape? Tune-up? Tone-down? Accommodate? Agree?

M **Modify** — To alter, to change the form or quality. Other color? Sound? Motion? Form? Size? Shape? Taste? Odor?

Magnify — To enlarge, to make greater in form or quality. Add what to make higher? Stronger? Thicker? Longer?

Minify — To make less, to minimize. Make what smaller? Lighter? Slower? Less frequent? Shrink? Reduce?

P **Put to Other Uses** — Use for purpose other than originally intended. Use when? How?

E **Eliminate** — To remove, omit, or get rid of a quality. What to cut out? Remove? Simplify? Weed out?

R **Reverse** — To make opposite or contrary. To turn what around? Upside down? Inside out? 180° flip?

Rearrange — Change order or sequence. Other pattern? Layout? Plan? Scheme? Regroup? Redistribute?

slowing down and turning off imaginative and creative expression. By nature, children possess a measure of ability to express wonderment, curiosity, imagination, and creativity. Early in life they discover that there are few payoffs in the reward system for this kind of activity. According to Dr. E. Paul Torrance, there is a measurable drop in the creative imaginative expression of children at the fourth and seventh grades. It appears that well-meaning adults, attempting to help children grow up and face reality, often dampen or extinguish the self-kindling fires of creative-imaginative thought and expression.

Dr. George Stoddard reminded us, "Creativity, the urge to inquire, to invent, and to perform has been stifled in millions of school children, now grown up, who did not get above rote learning, or did not stay above it." In this regard, Torrance noted, "Society is downright savage in its treatment of creative people, particularly when they are young." The opinions of experts culled from many sources seem to indicate that the great majority of the population has been caused to lay aside a valuable talent that could have helped them to become more self-sufficient, productive, and happier adults.

What, then, are these forces that seem to be drawn together in a well-organized campaign to stamp out creative imagination? It is believed that:

➤ Pressuring children to conform may very well be the major cause for the inhibition of creative-imaginative expression. Activities selected and goals set by adults, standardized home and school routines, controls exercised by clubs and organizations, and inflexible school curricula are examples of the repressing society in which the child lives.

➤ Domination by others and the threat of retaliation serve to choke off creative-imaginative response. To be told "That's a stupid idea" or "Why don't you grow up and act your age?" destroys feelings of self-worth and effectively blocks creative imagination.

➤ Imaginative thought and expression require playing around with ideas, toying with responsibilities, and roaming around in the world of make-believe. The nonacceptance of play attitudes, particularly in association with schoolwork, establishes a restrictive environment.

It is important to know about and to avoid conditions that block creative-imaginative expression. It is also important to know about attitudes and behaviors that encourage and reward this kind of intellectual activity. While serving as director for the National Schools

Project, Dr. Frank E. Williams and his colleagues developed and tested techniques designed to bring about creative-imaginative expression in children. It was found that the use of instructional strategies, which focused upon specific thinking abilities, and the establishment of classroom conditions, which encouraged the expression of particular kinds of feelings, produced statistically significant gains in the creative-imaginative expression of pupils. Many of Williams' strategies serve as the foundation for building the SCAMPER games that follow.

Thinking and Feeling Processes

Thinking Processes

Fluent Thinking consists of the generation of a quantity of ideas, plans, or products. The intent is to build a large store of information or material for selective use at a later time.

Flexible Thinking provides for shifts in categories of thought. It involves detours in thinking to include contrasting reasons, differing points of views, alternative plans, and the various aspects of a situation. A variety of kinds of ideas and differing approaches are considered. *Originality* is the production of unusual or unanticipated responses. It is characterized by uniqueness and novelty. Responses may be considered original if they are clever, remote, individualistic, uncommon, inventive, or creative in nature.

Elaborative Thinking is the ability to refine, embellish, or enrich an idea, plan, or product. It involves the addition of new and necessary details for clear and complete communication. It is an elegant response, an ornamented idea, or an adorned expansion upon things. Elaboration provides illuminating descriptive dimensions leaving very little to the imagination.

Feeling Processes

Curiosity is evidenced by inquisitiveness, a strong desire to know about something. It is exploratory behavior directed toward acquiring information. It involves the use of all of the senses to investigate, test out, and to confirm guesses and hunches about the unfamiliar or unknown.

Willingness to Take a Calculated Risk is activity that involves speculation, prediction, wisdom, and foresight. The probability of success and the chance of failure are estimated before action is taken. Risk taking is characterized by the will, disposition, and desire to set greater goals in anticipation of greater gains. Consideration for the elements of chance, liking the unknown, adventure, and a tolerance for insecurity are traits common to the risk taker. He or she also may be described as perceptive, inquiring, intuitive, and predictive.

Preference for Complexity is a willingness to accept a challenge. It represents a desire to wrestle with involved details, and an inclination to dig into knotty problems. Challenges may be in the form of intricate ideas, difficult problems, complex designs, or complicated theories. *Intuition* is a perceptive quality that involves quick and keen insight. It is a direct perception of truth or fact, independent of reasoning processes. It is the immediate apprehension of untaught knowledge.

Traditionally, children have been encouraged and have received rewards for: (a) learning that which has already been determined, (b) remembering that which is already known, and (c) conserving existing knowledge. It should be emphasized that the acquisition and retention of basic knowledge is a learning function necessary to the growth of the individual and should not be downgraded.

But, this is not the place to stop if intellectual potential is to be developed to the fullest. If children are to move closer to realizing their potential, they should be encouraged and given the opportunity to: (a) explore the undetermined, (b) revise that which is known, and (c) create what might be. There are many paths to human intellect, and play helps point the way. We should encourage students to walk down as many paths as possible on their day-to-day pursuit of knowledge and skills.

How to SCAMPER

It takes at least two people to SCAMPER, a child of 3 years or older, and an adult of any age. The adult, as game leader, may serve an individual child or a group number up to about 35. To play the games, the leader reads the script, paying close attention to the required pauses indicated by the three dots (. . .). The purpose of the pause is to provide time for the children to follow the cues and directions given. During the pause, the game leader should observe the emotions, reactions, and gestures of the players. Remember, the dots are your signal to wait and watch. You will know when to continue, usually when the players give a nod of approval, a smile, or other response. This is discussed further in the section titled "Introducing SCAMPER to Students."

A "Note to Game Leader" will precede some games. These additional instructions are particular to those games. Aside from these occasional notes, all of the text in each SCAMPER game is a full script to be read aloud to the players.

The games should be played with enthusiasm and expressed wonderment. This requirement places great responsibility on the leader. The leader, too, must be open to what might be, and willing to entertain extravagant and unrestrained ideas. An expression of enthusiasm sets the pace and establishes the emotional tone of the game. The success of the games clearly depend on the leader's ability and willingness to openly display an outpouring of warmth, enthusiasm, and positive expectation.

Within the structure of the games, ample opportunity is provided for the leader to exercise his or her own creative imagination. Games may be adapted for particular use. Leaders may wish to improvise or write their own games. Wide margins have been provided on the game pages; leaders may use this space to make notation of adaptations they wish to implement. Many suggestions for adaptation are included in Appendix A: SCAMPER on Your Own.

Before playing the games, it is recommended that the following procedure be followed:

➤ Read "Introducing SCAMPER to Students," and as you read, practice the expression you will use in giving the direction to the players. Imagine you are a child hearing the directions for the first time. How would you feel?

➤ Read the first two games as if you were actually playing with children. Take time to pause, pretend that you are a child, and envision the images that children will see when you lead them in this game. Timing yourself in this activity helps determine the actual time needed to play the game.

➤ Refer to Appendix A for suggestions on how to SCAMPER on Your Own, and adaptations that you may wish to use as a part of your game activity. The ideas suggested have been tried and found useful by classroom teachers. It is hoped that they will be of value to you and suggest new and original ideas that you will be able to put to use.

➤ It is good to recognize the attention span of the age group that will be playing. It can be expected that children in the 5–7-year-old age range will be able to focus attention on a game for about 10 minutes. Leaders have found it helpful to set and announce time limits before playing the games.

You are now ready to SCAMPER. Good luck! If all goes well, you will find that playing creative imagination games will lift you and your players to new heights of living and learning enjoyment.

Introducing SCAMPER to Students

We are going to play a game called SCAMPER. In playing the game, you will be asked to scamper about, but you won't really run around. This is a pretend game. When we pretend, we use our imagination. When you use your imagination, almost anything can happen. Making strange and unusual things happen in our imagination is fun. In playing the SCAMPER games, we hope to have fun. Here are the rules of the game. Listen while I read them to you.

Rules of the Game

I will tell you about something and ask you to think about it . . . to imagine and pretend. Sometimes, I will ask you to do something . . . you won't be expected to do it, but you can pretend that you are doing it. You know, just imagine that you are.

Remember, we are just pretending. Don't speak out when I ask you something. You may nod your head *yes* or shake your head *no*.

The best way to pretend is to put your hands over your eyes and close them, or to close your eyes and fold your arms in your lap. When you do this, you try to see and pretend to do what I am telling you.

Practice Game

· ·

➤ All right. Let's play a practice game.

➤ Are you ready? . . .

➤ Are your eyes closed? . . .

➤ Nod your head yes if you are ready and your eyes are closed . . .

➤ Good. Let's pretend that you have a dish of ice cream sitting right there on the table in front of you . . .

➤ Do you see it? . . .

➤ Nod your head yes if you see it . . .

➤ What flavor is it? Don't answer out loud. Just answer to yourself . . .

➤ Put a spoon on the table along side of the dish of ice cream . . .

➤ All right. Now, pick up the spoon and taste the ice cream . . .

➤ Is it good? . . .

➤ Go ahead and eat all of the ice cream in the dish . . .

➤ Is there any ice cream left in the dish? Shake your head no if it's all gone . . .

➤ Fine. Now open your eyes . . .

➤ Do you think that you know how to play the game? . . .

➤ Do you have any questions about playing the game? . . . (Take time to answer questions.)

I believe we are ready now, let's go ahead and play the first SCAMPER game.

Game 1:
Cardboard Box

Many kinds of things come in a cardboard box. Can you think of some? . . . You can take things out of a box, and you can put things into a box. Can you change a little box into a big box? . . . Can you change a box into a doghouse? . . . Sure you can, it isn't hard at all . . . if you use your imagination.

This game is called Cardboard Box. Close your eyes and we are ready to begin.

Pretend that you have a cardboard box about as big as a chair . . .

➤ Set it on the floor in front of you . . .

➤ Make it whatever size you want it to be . . .

➤ Make the box bigger and change the color . . .

Now, we are going to pretend that we are putting some things into the box. Think about the many different kinds of good things you could put into the box . . .

➤ Put them in . . .

➤ Keep putting things into the box until it is full . . .

➤ Now pile things on top . . .

➤ Keep piling things on top . . .

➤ Do you have things piled high? . . .

➤ Now, like magic, make everything in the box go away . . .

➤ Is the box empty? . . .

Take a long, flat box and put some wheels on it . . .

➤ Make it into a wagon . . .

➤ Have it be a red wagon . . .

➤ Jump into your red wagon and steer as it zips around the room . . .

➤ Stop the wagon and get out . . .

➤ Push it out the door . . .

Are you ready to make something else? . . .

➤ Take another box and make a doghouse . . .

➤ Put a dog in the doghouse . . .

➤ Make him brown with long hair . . .

➤ Give him a name . . .

➤ Call out his name and have him bark three times . . .

➤ Pet him and tell him he is a good dog . . .

➤ Give him some food and tell him goodbye . . .

Now take a wide, tall box and make a refrigerator . . .

➤ Put a door with hinges on it . . .

➤ Open the door . . .

➤ Did the light come on? . . .

➤ Put some shelves in the refrigerator . . .

➤ Put different kinds of vegetables on the shelves . . .

➤ Look at all of the food in the refrigerator and decide what you are going to have for lunch . . .

➤ Shut the door and come back when you're ready to fix lunch . . .

Get another box and we will make a space shuttle . . .

➤ Put a door and some windows in it . . .

➤ Get into your shuttle and shut the door . . .

➤ Get a little box and make a control panel with lights on it . . .

➤ Sit down in your seat and buckle the seat belt . . .

➤ Are you ready to go? . . .

➤ Grab the controls and push the button that starts the engines . . .

➤ Count down: 10, 9, 8, 7, 6, 5, 4, 3, 2, 1, 0, ignition, blast off . . .

➤ Look out the window . . .

➤ Is the Earth getting smaller? . . .

➤ Unbuckle your seat belt and float around in the cabin . . .

➤ Fly your shuttle around the moon . . .

➤ Take one more turn around the moon and head back to Earth . . .

➤ Start to slow it down for a landing . . .

➤ Set your shuttle down easy . . .

➤ Get out and walk around . . .

➤ Doesn't it feel good to be back on Earth? . . .

You can do all sorts of things with a cardboard box . . . if you use your imagination.

Game 2:

New Zoo

::: **Note to Game Leader**: It may be necessary to review the rules of the game before you start. For younger children, there is an alternate game that may be more suitable (see p. 16). :::

Some things seem to go well together. For example, peanut butter and jelly make good sandwiches. Milk and cereal are a good combination, but some kids like cereal without milk. Root beer and ice cream go together to make something that is different from either root beer or ice cream. Sometimes, we can combine things or parts of things that we do not usually think of as going together. When we do this, the results may be strange and interesting. It's possible to combine anything you want . . . when you use your imagination.

New Zoo is the name of this game. Can you guess what it's about? . . . If your eyes are closed, we are ready to play the game.

A moose has a big head and antlers, take a look at him . . .

➤ Do you see him? . . .

➤ Take his big head and antlers and put them on a hippopotamus . . .

➤ Think of a name that would describe this animal . . .

➤ Did you think of hippot-a-moose or moose-a-potamus? . . .

A kangaroo has big strong hind legs that help him jump . . .

➤ Give the kangaroo's hind legs to a donkey . . .

➤ Have this strange animal jump around on his hind legs . . .

➤ Think of a good name to describe this animal . . .

➤ You could call it donkey-roo or maybe even kang-a-donk . . .

Now look at a zebra . . .

➤ Can you see anything about this animal that makes him different from most other animals? . . .

➤ Remember what it is . . .

➤ Now look at a camel . . .

➤ Take the words that describe the characteristics of these two animals—stripes and hump—and combine them to make a name for your new animal . . .

➤ It could be a stripe-a-hump, hump-lines, or even humpster . . .

This time, choose any animal that you wish . . .

➤ Have you selected an animal? . . .

➤ Take a good look at her and notice any characteristics that tend to make her different from most other animals . . .

➤ Combine the words that describe the unique characteristics and make up a name for your new animal. We should be able to determine which two animals you chose by the name that you give your animal . . .

When we put things together we form strange and unusual combinations. Sometimes our unusual combinations may turn out to be something valuable.

We can try out all sorts of unusual combinations . . . if we are willing to use our imaginations.

Game 2 Alternate:
New Zoo

Note to Game Leader: The alternate game for younger children may be substituted after the kangaroo or the zebra sections. Continue playing using the following script:

A zebra has black and white stripes . . .

➤ Do you see them? . . .

➤ Put his stripes on a gorilla . . .

➤ Have the black and white striped gorilla walk around the room . . .

➤ Make up a new name to describe this animal . . .

➤ Do you have it? . . .

➤ Did you think of zeb-orilla? . . .

➤ How about gor-bra? . . .

A camel has a hump on her back . . .

➤ Do you see the camel with the hump? . . .

➤ Put the camel's hump on an elephant . . .

➤ Remember how she looks . . .

➤ Now, take the elephant's trunk and big ears and put them on a camel to make another animal . . .

➤ Do you have it? . . .

➤ All right, now take both of the animals that you have created and make a third animal that is different from either of the other two . . .

➤ Have you combined them? . . .

➤ Give this strange animal a name that will help to describe how she looks . . .

➤ Have you made up a new name? . . .

➤ Did you think of cam-el-phant? . . .

➤ How about ele-came-phant? . . .

Monkeys are cute animals that in some ways remind you of people . . .

➤ Take the head, tail, and fur coat of a monkey and put them on a cow . . .

➤ Invent a new name to describe this unusual animal . . .

➤ Have you thought of one? . . .

➤ How about monk-cow? . . .

A goose has a long neck and brown and white feathers . . .

➤ Take his long neck and white feathers and put them on a grizzly bear . . .

➤ Give this animal a name . . .

➤ Would goo-bear be a good name? . . .

➤ Maybe you would prefer grizz-neck . . .

When we put things together we come up with combinations that make new things. Sometimes our ideas for combining things may turn out to be valuable.

We can try out all sorts of unusual combinations . . . if we are willing to use our imaginations.

Game 3:

Doughnuts

I suppose that there is really nothing more wonderful than a doughnut, especially when you are hungry. You could eat doughnuts all day long if you had enough of them. You could eat them all night long if you could stay awake. Doughnuts are usually round, but they don't have to be. You could make a square doughnut if you wanted to. In fact, you could make a birthday cake out of a doughnut . . . if you used your imagination.

Let's pretend that we have a plate piled with doughnuts sitting here on a table . . .

➤ Do you see them? . . .

➤ How many doughnuts do you think are piled on that plate? . . .

➤ Take a guess . . .

➤ Now count them to be sure . . .

➤ How many are there? . . .

Good! Now think of all the good things that you could put inside a doughnut to make it taste better. Go ahead and think about your choices . . .

➤ How many different kinds of things did you think of? . . .

➤ Now think of some strange and unusual kinds of things you could put inside a doughnut . . .

➤ Try to think of something that no one else would think of . . .

➤ Did you think of some unusual things? . . .

Let's pretend that we have a squirt gun for putting things inside doughnuts. I am going to name some things that we could squirt inside of a doughnut. If you thought of any of these things nod your head when I call it out. Are you ready? . . .

➤ Peanut butter . . .

➤ Take the squirter and put some peanut butter in a doughnut . . .

➤ Take a bite and squish it around in your mouth . . .

➤ Do you like peanut butter doughnuts? . . .

➤ Did you think about chocolate pudding? . . .

➤ Squirt some chocolate pudding in a doughnut . . .

➤ Take a bite . . .

➤ Is it good? . . .

Now let's make some doughnuts that are not round . . .

➤ Make them without holes . . .

➤ Make one that looks like a loaf of bread . . .

➤ Make one as thin as a pencil . . .

➤ Make a doughnut that looks like a pretzel . . .

➤ Make one the size of a baseball . . .

➤ Make one as big as a house . . .

Let's pretend that we have a doughnut house . . .

➤ Put a swimming pool where the hole in the doughnut would be . . .

➤ Fill the swimming pool with applesauce . . .

➤ Walk around your doughnut house . . .

➤ Does it smell good in the house? . . .

➤ Rub your hands on the ceiling . . .

➤ How does it feel? . . .

➤ Take a bite of the floor . . .

➤ How does it taste? . . .

➤ Now run out and jump into the pool . . .

➤ What kind of sound did it make when you jumped into the pool? . . .

➤ Go back into the house and take a grape juice shower . . .

Did you ever decorate a doughnut? . . .

➤ Think of all of the things, all of the colors, all of the designs you could put on doughnuts . . .

➤ Imagine that you are going to decorate a doughnut for a special purpose. We want to decorate the doughnuts so that everyone will know exactly what they are for . . .

➤ First, make a Halloween doughnut . . .

➤ What are you going to put on it? . . .

➤ Would everyone know what it is for? . . .

➤ Now make a Valentine doughnut . . .

➤ What shape is it? . . .

➤ What colors did you put on it? . .

➤ Did you put anything into it? . . .

➤ Make a Fourth of July doughnut . . .

➤ Make a birthday cake doughnut . . .

➤ Put enough candles on it for your next birthday . . .

➤ Light the candles . . .

➤ Make a wish . . .

➤ Blow out the candles . . .

➤ Did you blow them all out? . . .

You can do just about anything you want with doughnuts . . . if you use your imagination.

Game 4:

Stuffed Animals

Have you ever played with a teddy bear? . . . Most of the older people you know played with teddy bears when they were children. Teddy bears are stuffed animals that are fun to play with. They have big eyes and ears and soft, fuzzy fur. They stay put when you set them down and seldom get lost. Have you ever thought what it would be like if toy animals decided to walk around? . . . Wouldn't it be fun if toy animals could play hide and seek with you? . . . Stuffed animals can do all kinds of unusual things . . . if you use your imagination. In this next game you are going to see, hear, and feel thought pictures about stuffed animals.

Sit down on the floor and place a stuffed pony in front of you . . .

➤ Give him black and white silky fur . . .

➤ Rub your hand over this silky fur . . .

➤ Put your hand on his cold, wet nose . . .

➤ Doesn't it feel funny? . . .

➤ Put a battery in so that his eyes light up when you pull his tail . . .

➤ Pull his tail and have his eyes light up . . .

➤ Do it again . . .

➤ Put a wind-up box in him so he can sing when you turn him on . . .

➤ Wind him up, turn him on, and have him sing a cowboy song . . .

Now let's play with a white, stuffed polar bear . . .

➤ Make him about the size of a loaf of bread . . .

➤ Take a pretty blue ribbon and tie a little bell around his neck . . .

➤ Have him walk around the room . . .

➤ Have the bell ring as he walks around the room . . .

➤ Tell him to stop walking and sit up on his hind legs . . .

➤ Ask him to stick out his big red tongue . . .

➤ Did he do it? . . .

➤ Have him go over to the corner and lie down . . .

Now let's play with a penguin . . .

➤ Penguins are black and white, but let's make ours red and green . . .

➤ Take a good look at our red and green penguin . . .

➤ Make him a happy penguin that smiles and rolls his eyes around . . .

➤ Make him a jumping penguin that jumps like a kangaroo . . .

➤ Have him jump around a bit . . .

➤ Put him against the wall next to the polar bear . . .

Now we are going to have a parade of the stuffed animals . . .

➤ Have the black and white, singing pony lead the parade . . .

➤ Next in line is the polar bear with his bell ringing . . .

➤ Put some roller skates on him and have him follow the pony . . .

➤ Next is the penguin, smiling and rolling his eyes around as he jumps along behind the polar bear . . .

➤ Now pretend that you are a little white rabbit with big blue eyes . . .

➤ Get into the parade right behind the red and green penguin . . .

➤ Have all of the animals march around the room . . .

➤ Have them go around the room one more time and then stop against the wall . . .

Stuffed animals can do all kinds of fun and unusual things . . . when you use your imagination.

Game 5:

Sticks

A toothpick is made out of wood, and so is a baseball bat. You could call them both sticks if you wanted to. Sticks come in all shapes and sizes. They also have different colors and sometimes smell or feel differently. Hardly anyone pays much attention to sticks because there are so many of them around. But, if people really take the time to look at a stick, they might see some unusual things . . . particularly if they use their imaginations. In this game, we are going to work wonders with plain old sticks.

Take a stick about as long as your arm . . .

➤ Make it an old, weatherworn stick with the bark off . . .

➤ Make it crooked with knots in it . . .

➤ Make it rough . . .

➤ Make it gray . . .

➤ Do you have it? . . .

➤ All right. Hold it out at arm's length and pretend that it's a snake . . .

➤ Have it wiggle and stick out its tongue . . .

➤ Hand it to someone and tell him it is a snake . . .

➤ Watch to see what it does . . .

➤ Tell him to turn the snake loose in the grass . . .

Take another stick . . .

➤ Make it about half as long as your arm . . .

➤ Do you have it? . . .

➤ Fine. Stand it up on a base and put it in the center of the table . . .

➤ Good. Spray gold paint on it . . .

➤ Touch it up if it needs it . . .

➤ Pretend that there is a motor in the base that will make the stick turn slowly . . .

➤ Turn it on . . .

➤ Turn it off . . .

➤ Stick some red colored jewels on the gold stick . . .

➤ Put some yellow jewels on it . . .

➤ Put some black jewels on it . . .

➤ Put some other colored jewels on it . . .

➤ Turn a spotlight on the jeweled stick . . .

➤ Push the button that will make the stick turn around slowly . . .

➤ Step back and watch the jeweled stick turn slowly on the table . . .

➤ Turn it off and walk away . . .

Find another old stick about as long as your favorite book is tall . . .

➤ Have it be as round as your wrist . . .

➤ Do you have it? . . .

➤ Very well. Now we are going to make an old man puppet . . .

➤ First, take a pencil and draw a face on one end of the stick . . .

➤ Take some string and put white hair on the end of the stick around the face . . .

➤ Get some pieces of cloth and put a shirt and pants on him . . .

➤ Find something that you could use for shoes . . .

➤ Did you find something? . . .

➤ Put some shoes on him . . .

➤ Tie some strings up and down and have him walk around . . .

➤ Put him up on the shelf . . .

Now we are going to make a stick animal . . .

➤ To do this, you really will have to use your imagination and do some original thinking . . .

➤ Are you ready? . . .

➤ Take another old stick any size or shape that you want . . .

➤ Do you have it? . . .

➤ First, we will need to give it a head . . .

➤ Think of all the things that you might use for eyes, ears, nose, and mouth . . .

➤ Now find something that you could use for legs . . .

➤ Do you want her to have a tail? . . .

➤ If you do, put it on . . .

➤ We forgot to put on fur, skin, or feathers. Which do you want to use? . . .

➤ Put it on . . .

➤ Look her over from all sides . . .

➤ Does she need anything else? . . .

➤ If she does, put it on . . .

➤ How does she look now? . . .

➤ Give her a name and stand her on the shelf . . .

➤ What name did you give her? . . .

The next time you are out walking, see if you can find an old stick. If you do, take a good look at it. You may find it reminds you of something.

Remember, an old stick can be anything . . . if you use your imagination.

Alphabet Cake

Did you ever eat cake for breakfast? . . . How about a pancake . . . If we were to list all of the different kinds of cake that we know about, we would have a long list. Think about all of the kinds of cake that you have eaten at one time or another . . . If you wanted to invent a new kind of cake it wouldn't be too hard. In making a cake you can put things into it, on top of it, or around it. You also could make it different shapes and sizes. In this game we are going to try our hand at inventing new kinds of cake. Some silly things may happen, but then again we might get some good, new ideas . . . when we use our imagination.

In playing this game we are going to take the letters of the alphabet and use them to remind us of new kinds of cake we could make . . .

➤ Let's start with the first letter of the alphabet and see if we can think of some things that begin with the letter A. Think of things that we could put on or into a cake . . .

➤ Let's try applesauce. We could put applesauce into the cake when we baked it or we could spread it on top for frosting . . .

➤ Here's another idea. Asparagus begins with the letter A. Let's see what we might be able to do with asparagus . . .

➤ We could chop up asparagus and put it into the cake before we baked it. We might even take some asparagus juice and use it to flavor the frosting . . .

➤ We could put some sticks of asparagus on top of the cake like candles or we could place asparagus sticks along side of the cake for decoration . . .

➤ Do you think you would like asparagus cake? . . .

Let's try the letter B. Search around in your mind and see if you can see some things that begin with the letter B. Look for all kinds of things that you might use to make a new kind of cake . . .

➤ Have you thought of some things that begin with the letter B? . . .

➤ Take some of these things and make a cake . . .

➤ Do you have it finished? . . .

➤ Set it over on the table . . .

➤ Is it really a different kind of cake? . . .

➤ Did anyone put bologna on his or her cake? . . .

Try to think of some foods that begin with the letter C.

➤ Think of more things you can eat that begin with the letter C . . .

➤ Take some of these things and make another cake . . .

➤ Does it look good? . . .

➤ Take a bite and see how it tastes . . .

➤ Do you like it? . . .

➤ Did anyone use chili? . . .

➤ How about catsup? . . .

➤ Did anyone use carrots or cabbage? . . .

You may run through the alphabet as far as children are willing to go, or you may wish to randomly assign alphabet letters and let the children work on their cakes individually.

It's fun to invent new kinds of cakes, and easy too . . . if you use your imagination.

Game 7:

Crazy

Note to Game Leader: This game calls for a high degree of abstract thinking on the part of the players. It may be necessary to provide extra time for the players to visualize the cues. Once a cue is given, it may be desirable to repeat it after a short pause.

As an optional activity, the leader may say, "Now what do you think of that?" When this cue is given by the leader, pupils may respond, "Say, that's really crazy." Note cues in bold type throughout the game. Instruct players of the cue to be given and their expected response before starting the games.

Other optional activities may be found in the Appendix A: SCAMPER on Your Own.

SCAMPER games are designed to help you see pictures in your mind. Sometimes, we call these pictures *think pictures*. The think pictures that you see might be about something that could really be true. But then again, they might be about something crazy that could hardly ever be true. Crazy things are fun. We like to think about crazy things and sometimes we like to do crazy things.

Once again, I will ask you to think about something and to try to see what it is I am describing . . . When you see it and are ready to move on, nod your head yes . . . All right. Let's begin . . .

➤ Candy bars are made of soap . . .

➤ A green and yellow donkey is climbing a rope . . .

➤ Stars in the sky are like pine trees . . .

➤ Chimpanzees look just like me . . .

➤ **Now what do you think of that? . . .**

➤ **Say, that's really crazy . . .**

You are wearing your clothes turned inside out . . .

➤ Jump on an idea and ride it about . . .

➤ Monkeys stumble in a candy cane jungle . . .

➤ Witches and goblins are very humble . . .

➤ **Now what do you think of that? . . .**

➤ **Say, that's really crazy . . .**

Sunbeams make jet trails in the sky . . .

➤ A hairy ape is eating apple pie . . .

➤ Colored balloons grow wild in a patch of briar . . .

➤ The bottom of the ocean grows higher and higher . . .

➤ **Now what do you think of that? . . .**

➤ **Say, that's really crazy . . .**

The moon beams down like a circus clown . . .

➤ Hands on the clock wave up and down . . .

➤ A house goes jogging down the street . . .

➤ Tigers put catsup on hamburgers they eat . . .

➤ **Now what do you think of that? . . .**

➤ **Say, that's really crazy . . .**

Marshmallow trees bend at the knees . . .

➤ A dog catcher chases birds and bees . . .

➤ Black snow sifts down like lumps of coal . . .

➤ Basketballs shoot players through the hoop . . .

➤ **Now what do you think of that? . . .**

➤ **Say, that's really crazy . . .**

We can do many interesting, crazy things when we see think pictures and . . . use our imagination.

Game 8:

Light Bulb

We have so many wonderful things to help us live comfortably that we really don't give much thought about it. But if somebody hadn't given some thought to these things, they would have never been invented. Have you ever thought what it would be like if light bulbs had never been invented? . . . I wouldn't like that, would you? . . . Light bulbs help in many ways. But I think we could make them even better than they are now. I'm sure we could make them better . . . if we use our imagination.

Put a light bulb in your left hand . . .

➤ Hold it out in front of you . . .

➤ Very good. Now we are going to ask the light bulb to do whatever it is that we wish it to do. You may wish very hard for the light bulb to get your message, but let's try it and see if the light bulb will do what we desire it to do . . .

➤ Wish for the light bulb to turn on . . .

➤ Is it on? . . .

➤ Turn it off . . .

Now let's have the light bulb shine different colors . . .

➤ What color do you desire? Red? Green? Blue? Orange? Is there any color you desire? . . .

➤ Wish for the light bulb to shine whatever color you want it to . . .

➤ Did it shine your color? . . .

➤ Would you rather the bulb shine warm or cold? . . .

➤ Take your choice and have the light bulb shine the way you want it to . . .

➤ Do you feel the temperature changing in the room? . . .

➤ Put the light bulb aside . . .

Get another light bulb and unscrew the bottom of it . . .

➤ Take the bottom off and pour in some mosquito spray . . .

➤ Screw the bottom back on . . .

➤ Hold it out in front of you and wish for it to start shining . . .

➤ As it shines have it kill all of the mosquitoes . . .

Now make the light bulb bigger and flat like a television screen . . .

➤ Blink your eyes and have a program come on . . .

➤ Blink your eyes and change the picture to another program . . .

➤ Blink them for another program . . .

➤ Now blink your eyes and have Saturday's cartoons come on . . .

➤ Are you going to be happy next Saturday? . . .

➤ Blink your eyes and turn off the TV . . .

Take another light bulb. Make it about half as big as it is now . . .

➤ Let's pretend that it is a magic flashlight . . .

➤ Shine it at a cat and make the cat as small as a mouse . . .

➤ Shine it on a mouse and make the mouse as big as a cat . . .

➤ Have the mouse chase the cat . . .

➤ Shine it on the dog and have the dog meow like a cat . . .

➤ Shine it on a bird and have the bird bark like a dog . . .

➤ Shine it on a cow and have the cow grunt like a pig . . .

➤ Shine it on a pig and have the pig sing like a bird . . .

➤ Put your magic light bulb on the shelf . . .

Now put a light bulb in each hand . . .

➤ Hold your arms out straight to the side . . .

➤ Pretend the light bulbs are jet engines. Run down the street for a take-off . . .

➤ Run faster . . .

➤ Zoom yourself up into the air . . .

➤ Higher . . .

➤ Circle over your house . . .

➤ Look down . . .

➤ Do you see anyone you know? . . .

➤ Now zoom over town and look down . . .

➤ Do you see any stores? . . .

➤ Zoom away from town and look down at the river . . .

➤ Zoom away and look at the mountains . . .

➤ Look at the ocean . . .

➤ Zoom back toward home . . .

➤ When you are over your house, let go of the light bulbs and have them zip away into space . . .

➤ Open your parachute and float slowly to the ground . . .

➤ As you float down, look all around you . . .

➤ You are heading toward your backyard . . .

➤ Touch your feet down, take off your parachute, and go tell everyone that you are home . . .

➤ I'll bet you never thought you could make a jet plane out of light bulbs . . .

Nothing is very hard to do . . . if you use your imagination.

What in the World Did You Find?

When we lose something, we usually feel bad about it. But if we lose a cold, we feel good. When we lose something, we hope that someone will find it and return it to us. If we find something that someone else has lost, we should try to find the owner and return it to him or her. If we go looking for ideas, we can keep whatever ideas we find. It isn't hard to find ideas . . . if you are willing to use your imagination.

In this game, we are going to search all around the world to see what we might find. Remember we are just making believe. We are pretending that something is lost and we are going to look for it. We don't know what it is, what it looks like, or where it was lost. When you are pretending, you can find just about anything you want.

Close your eyes and let's start our imaginary search . . .

➤ First, let's look in your house . . .

➤ Look for some places where something could be hidden . . .

➤ Do you see some places where something might get lost? . . .

Walk all through the house; go into every room and look around . . .

➤ Did you see some places where something could get lost? . . .

➤ Go out the back door and look all around outside . . .

➤ Do you see some places where something might get lost? . . .

Now pretend that a helicopter is coming down in your yard . . .

➤ Do you see it? . . .

➤ Jump in and tell the pilot where you want him to take you . . .

➤ Tell the pilot to take you any place in the world you want to go . . .

➤ You are on your way . . .

Now you are there . . .

➤ Look all around . . .

➤ Look for some places where something could get lost . . .

➤ Now think of some more strange and unusual places in the world where something might get lost . . .

➤ Of all of the places that you have thought of, pick out the one place that you believe is the most unusual, one that you are sure no one could ever guess . . .

➤ Do you have it? . . .

➤ All right. That place is where you found something . . .

➤ Remember where it is and we'll go to another part of the game . . .

We don't know what you found yet, do we? . . . Whatever it might turn out to be, it will have to look like something . . .

➤ We will need to choose some words that will help us describe it to other people. First, we will look at all the colors that it might be . . .

➤ Search in your mind and try to see all of the colors that you know about . . .

➤ Put them on a wheel and have the wheel spin around in front of you . . .

➤ Do you see all of the colors spinning around? . . .

➤ Choose two or three colors that you like best . . .

➤ Make them into a pattern or design . . .

➤ Make a design with squares in it . . .

➤ Make a design with stripes . . .

➤ Make a design with dots in it . . .

➤ Remember the colors and design . . .

Besides color and design, there are other things we might wish to consider when we describe something . . .

➤ Think about all of the ways something might feel if you touched it . . .

➤ Did you think of hot, cold, soft, rough, sticky, or smooth? . . .

➤ Think of all of the sounds it might make if you dropped it, hit it, or wound it up . . .

➤ It could be big, round, small, or flat . . .

➤ What other shapes or sizes could it be . . .

➤ It could taste like pickles or pears . . .

➤ What are some of the tastes that you like? . . .

➤ Are there some tastes you don't like? . . .

You have thought of a large number of ideas to describe something, something you might find. As you select some of these descriptions, don't worry if they seem silly when we put them together. All right . . . Think back and remember the color and design that you selected . . .

➤ Select some words that describe how something might feel . . .

➤ Choose some words that would describe the size and shape of something . . .

➤ What words will describe the sounds something might make? . . .

➤ Now see the description you have selected as I call them out . . .

➤ Color and design . . .

➤ How it feels . . .

➤ Sounds . . .

➤ Size and shape . . .

➤ Taste . . .

➤ Try to remember your description . . .

➤ Have you wondered what it is that you are describing? . . .

➤ You will find out in the next part of the game . . .

You already have decided where it is that something is lost. You also have determined what it looks like and other ways to describe it. The next thing you will need to do is find out exactly what it is you found.

First, it would be good for you to realize that just about anything could be lost and that you could find it. You could find a lost dog, a lost gold mine, or a lost astronaut. You could find a lost birthday present, or a lost school bus. Go ahead and picture in your mind all of the lost things that you could possibly find...

➤ Think of many different kinds of things ...

➤ See some unusual things ...

➤ See some things that no one else will think of ...

➤ Of all of the things that you were able to see, pick out the one thing that would be different from what anyone else might choose...

➤ Do you have it? ...

➤ All right. That is what you found ...

Think back, do you remember where you found it? ...

➤ Do you remember the descriptive words? ...

➤ What color and design? ...

➤ How does it feel? ...

➤ What sounds does it make? ...

➤ What size and shape? ...

➤ Does it have a taste? ...

Put these things together so that you can answer the question, "What in the world did you find?" You can find some very unusual things ... if you use your imagination.

Repmacs

Do you have any Repmacs around your house? . . . You don't really know, do you? You can't have an idea about Repmacs or anything else unless you have seen, heard, felt, or tasted it. The things that help us to know more about something are called traits, characteristics, or attributes. They help us to know what something is like. When we look real close to see what something is like, we may get an idea about using it for other things. Repmacs are things that we make out of something else. It will help you to know more about Repmacs if I give you some examples.

If a safety pin reminded you of a fish hook and you decided to bend the pin and make a fish hook, it would be a Repmacs. You made the fish hook from something else. If you made a parachute out of a handkerchief, it would be a Repmacs. If you used a pencil to dial a telephone, it would be a Repmacs. Repmacs are inventions. It's fun to be an inventor, and easy, too . . . if you use your imagination.

Find the lid from an old garbage can . . .

➤ Close your eyes and try to see the garbage can lid . . .

➤ Turn it upside down, fasten a stick to it, and put it in the yard for a bird bath . . .

➤ Find the lids from two old garbage cans . . .

➤ Grab the handles and march down the street clashing them like cymbals . . .

Now take a wire coat hanger . . .

➤ Bend it into all kinds of shapes . . .

➤ Bend it into the shape of a heart . . .

➤ Put some red ribbon or colored paper on it and make a Valentine decoration . . .

Set a tin can on the table . . .

➤ Take a good look at it . . .

➤ What is it like? . . .

➤ Does it remind you of anything else? . . .

➤ Could you use it for anything if it were turned upside down? . . .

➤ What could you do with it if both the bottom and the top of the can were removed? . . .

➤ What would it be used for if you made it bigger? . . .

➤ If you made it smaller? . . .

➤ If you changed the shape? . . .

What could you use the can for if you painted it? . . .

➤ Put colored cloth on it? . . .

➤ Tied wire to it? . . .

➤ Punched holes in it? . . .

➤ Filled it full of cement? . . .

➤ Cut it into strips? . . .

➤ Made it smell good? . . .

➤ Made it out of chocolate? . . .

➤ Made it disappear when you wanted it to? . . .

➤ Put rocks in it and put the lid back on? . . .

Now, see if you can make some Repmacs on your own . . .

➤ What could you make out of the top of an old ironing board? . . .

➤ Try to see an old ironing board as part of something . . .

➤ What could you do to an empty plastic container so that it could be used for something else? . . .

➤ Make it into something else . . .

➤ If you had hundreds of used Valentine cards, what could you do with them? . . .

➤ What different kinds of things could you use them for? . . .

Repmacs is the name of this book spelled backwards. In our imagination we can perform operations on things and make them different. For example, we can substitute something for another thing, or we can combine one thing with another. Sometimes, we can adapt or change it to make it serve another purpose. We can make a thing bigger, smaller, or change its shape. We can use a thing for another purpose than originally intended and we can remove parts of it if we want to. And then also, we can arrange its parts or reverse the position of a thing or turn it around.

You can invent, compose, and create, if you SCAMPER . . . and you use imagination.

Eighth Day of the Week

"**T**here are not enough days in the week!" Did you ever hear anyone say that? If so, that person was saying that there is not enough time to do what he or she wants to do or needs to do. If we use our imagination, there might be a way to solve that problem. Let's pretend that there are eight days in every week. The extra day would come after Sunday and before Monday. The eighth day would have to have a name. It might work to use a name that describes the things we would do on that day. Let's try it and see what happens.

Dream along and make a day that you would spend with others. In your mind, think of people who you would like to be with . . .

➤ Now that you have some people in mind, choose some of them to be with you on the eighth day of the week . . .

➤ Fine. Now that you have some people to spend time with you, you will need to think of things that all of you would like to do together. Think of those things . . .

➤ See yourself and your friends doing those things . . .

➤ We'll call it Friends Day.

Here's another idea. Let's say that the eighth day of the week is set aside to go to places that we want to go. That would be a great idea. Think of all the places in the world that you would like to visit, then narrow it down to one place . . .

➤ Do you have it? . . . Good! Now get on an airplane, settle back, and enjoy your flight. You are above the clouds flying along . . .

➤ Your plane is now coming in for a landing . . .

➤ Leave the plane, walk around, meet people, and go shopping and sightseeing . . .

➤ Your visit is over. Get aboard the plane and get ready to fly home. You are now flying along and heading home . . .

➤ It touches down . . .

➤ You are now back home. Today is Fly Day.

It has turned out to be a very warm day. You really should go outdoors and enjoy the sunshine. There are many things to do outside on a warm, sunshiny day.

➤ Make a list in your mind of things to do . . .

➤ You have all day to do these things. Choose some of them, and then see yourself doing them . . .

➤ Better take time out now for a cold drink. Pretend that you have a cool drink. Sip it slowly and enjoy it . . .

➤ What day is it? Of course, it's Thirst Day.

Remember, we said that the eighth day of the week could be spent doing things that we didn't get done the first seven days. Think back. What are some things that didn't get done? . . .

➤ You could do them now in your imagination. Find something to do, and do it in your imagination . . .

➤ Do you feel better now that you have gotten it out of the way? You can get caught up any old When's Day.

Today is Two's Day. Everything happens in two's.

➤ Sit down for breakfast and eat two of everything . . .

➤ Have a happy Two's Day.

Today is your day to do nothing—nothing, but sit in your yard dreaming and listening to the sounds around you.

➤ About half asleep, you hear the birds singing . . .

➤ Down the block a dog is barking . . .

➤ Across town a church bell is ringing . . .

➤ A kitten jumps up beside you, brushes your face, and purrs in your ear . . .

➤ The sounds of nature are all around you . . .

➤ Listen, do you hear that siren? . . .

➤ It is coming closer . . .

➤ It turns down your street . . .

➤ Jump up and see what is happening . . .

➤ You knew it all the time, it's Sounds Day.

There are many things that have a pleasing aroma. To name a few you might mention perfume, bread baking in the oven, or a bouquet of flowers.

➤ Think of things that have a pleasing aroma, as you place them one by one on a long table . . .

➤ Think hard and place some more things on the long table . . .

➤ Now you have a smellgasboard. Starting at the front of the line, take a whiff of everything as you go along the line . . .

➤ What else? It's Smells Day!

You can make a new day for any occasion . . . if you use your imagination.

Follow-Up Activities

➤ Call on players to invent their own "eighth day of the week" and then write a game scenario.

➤ Selecting any one of the day titles, call on students to use it as a title for a rhyme or poem.

Game 12:

Sights and Sounds, Upside Down, and All Around

Note to Game Leader: It is likely that game leaders will not wish to use all of the many parts of this game in one session. It is recommended that you be selective and group the parts for two or more sessions.

When you want it to, your mind can work magic. You can direct your mind to think about something that happened years ago. If you try, you can see a picture in your mind of the things that happened. If you wish, you can direct your mind to the future. When you do, you are able to think about and see images of events that might happen 5 to 10 years from now. When you turn the magic on, you also are able to see and hear things that may never happen. Turn your magic on and see some things that may never happen.

➤ Back and forth swim the fish in the sea . . .
   Watch as they decorate their Christmas tree . . .

➤ Your breakfast food box is full of prunes . . .
   Open the flap and it plays a tune . . .

➤ Both boys and girls have yellow curls . . .
   They shake their heads and a flag unfurls . . .

➤ Off you go for a walk in the sky . . .
   Stop at the corner for a burger and fries . . .

➤ Cats and rats are very fat . . .
   They are dressed in clothes and wearing hats . . .

➤ Rivers are yellow, then green, then brown . . .
Fill your glass with soda and drink it down . . .

➤ The birds you see will flutter and fly . . .
Then stop at traffic signals in the sky . . .

➤ Turn on the TV set that is in your head . . .
Watch your favorite program while lying in bed . . .

➤ Take a space ship out of your pocket . . .
Send it flying like a rocket . . .

➤ Dogs and hogs are spinning a log . . .
Put them on land and send them to jog . . .

➤ What you think will turn to stone . . .
At the end of the day a mountain has grown . . .

➤ Look around for a place to hide . . .
No place to go, so vanish inside . . .

➤ Doughnuts are square and full of air . . .
Two dollars a dozen at the county fair . . .

➤ You are going up, up, up, in a hot air balloon . . .
Your pilot is a hairy baboon . . .

➤ Look in a mirror and see a frown . . .
Notice your eyeballs are hanging down . . .

➤ The wumbas and wampas come walking by . . .
Give them wings and teach them to fly . . .

➤ Your favorite meal is on the table . . .
Feed it to the horse out in the stable . . .

➤ Listen close and bells will chime . . .
Listen far and words will rhyme. . .

➤ With vision and hope for good times ahead . . .
The sun will beam down on your pretty head . . .

You can experience a world of adventures . . . if you use your imagination.

Follow-Up Activities

➤ Organize players in groups of two. As games are repeated, partners take turns describing aloud, and in great detail, the visions that they are experiencing. Players may be given the opportunity to call for games of their choice.

➤ Working in small groups, or in a large group, players may be asked to tell what led up to the game event. Other players then may be asked to tell what happened as a result of the event.

Brown Paper Bags

What is it that you bring home from the store, never eat, and end up throwing away? . . . The answer is brown paper grocery bags. Brown paper bags are useful, but they are dull and not very exciting. It would pep up our day if grocery bags were made in bright colors.

Let's try that idea in our imagination. Pretend that a brown paper bag is sitting on the table in front of you . . .

➤ Do you see it? Good. Take another look at the brown bag . . .

➤ Now make your bag a friendly orange color . . .

➤ Make it a cheerful green color . . .

➤ Make it a peppy yellow color . . .

➤ What would a friendly, cheerful, peppy bag look like? Make your bag look just like that . . .

Using our imagination, we can pretend and do many wonderful things with a paper bag. First, let's make some improvements . . .

➤ To start, put a handle on it . . .

➤ Give it a lid or a cover . . .

➤ Put a flap pocket on the side . . .

➤ Put your name on it in big black letters . . .

➤ Make a place for a radio in the handle . . .

➤ Give it three bright colors, then stand back and look at it...

➤ Are there any improvements you would like to make on your bag? If so, go ahead and make them...

➤ Now, how do you like your bag?...

Take another brown bag. On the side of it write Bother Bag. You will use the Bother Bag to collect things that give you trouble. You also might wish to collect things that are worn out, broken, too small, or anything you wish to get rid of.

➤ Now, one by one, see the things you want to put in the bag, then put them in...

➤ Keep putting things that bother you into the bag...

➤ Now pick up the Bother Bag and shake it...

➤ The bag is empty. The things that bothered you and gave you trouble have disappeared...

➤ Make a place for a radio in the handle...

➤ Give it three bright colors, then stand back and look at it...

➤ Are there any improvements you would like to make on your bag? If so, go ahead and make them...

➤ Now, how do you like your bag?...

Take another brown bag and write on it Boodle Bag. In the bag you will collect a boodle of things that you wish for. One by one make a wish for something. Then, reach in the Boodle Bag and pull it out.

➤ Start wishing...

➤ The bag is not empty; keep on wishing and pulling things out of the bag...

➤ Isn't it wonderful, the things you can do with your imagination?...

Going on, there are some improvements we can make on the brown paper bag. First, make it a heavy-duty, strong, white plastic bag...

➤ Look at the bag now...

➤ Make it air tight and water tight...

➤ Make it much larger...

➤ Make it much smaller...

➤ Turn it inside out, and use scissors to cut around the open end to make a fringe . . .

➤ Pretend you have made the bag into a white-fringed rain hat . . . and see how it looks . . .

Using your imagination, you can create all kinds of things out of a white plastic bag. I will name some things. Your task will be to make them out of a plastic bag and see them in your imagination. Ready? . . .

➤ Make a rain coat for a dog . . .

➤ Make a trampoline and bounce on it . . .

➤ Make a kite and fly it . . .

➤ Put a handle on it and make a fly swatter . . .

➤ Make a shade and put it on a lamp . . .

➤ Make a parachute and float down to earth . . .

➤ Make a poster and hang it on the wall . . .

➤ Buy some goldfish and carry them home in your bag . . .

A white plastic bag is a neat thing to have. You can make many kinds of things out of a white plastic bag. Now it is your turn to think of some things to make out of the bag, and to find some new ways of using it. In what ways might you use the bag if you were going for a hike in the woods? Think of some ways and see them in your imagination . . .

➤ Do it now . . .

➤ Ways to use it in the kitchen? . . .

➤ Ways to use it with pets? . . .

➤ Ways to use it with sports? . . .

➤ Ways to use it on a picnic? . . .

➤ If you think of other ways to use the bag, write them down so you don't forget them. You may have a valuable idea.

A plain bag from the store can contain anything you wish . . . if you use your imagination.

Follow-Up Activities

➤ Conduct a discussion in which players tell the uses they made of the plastic bag.

➤ Using a bag, brick, tin can, or coat hanger, apply each step of the SCAMPER technique in a brainstorm for other uses.

Dogs and Cats and Hogs and Bats

I n this game, you will use your magic mind viewer. When you look into your viewer, like magic you will see a picture of those things that you bring into your mind. The pictures you see will be in color and very clear. The harder you try to see the colored picture, the clearer it will be. Are you ready to try out your magic mind viewer? Fine, let's get started.

Looking into your viewer you will see a picture of a dog. It can be any kind of dog that you want to make it . . .

➤ Look now and see a dog . . .

➤ Now that you have a picture of a dog, look to see what it is that makes this animal different from other animals . . .

➤ Do you have it? . . .

➤ Remember it . . .

Next, look into your viewer and see a cat. Make it any kind of cat that you wish to make it . . .

➤ Look now and see the cat . . .

➤ Next, we wish to see what it is that makes this animal different from all other kinds of animals . . .

➤ Look now to see the ways in which it is different . . .

➤ Remember what it is that makes the cat different . . .

If you were to visit a farm, you might see a hog. If you look now, you will see a hog in your viewer . . .

➤ Look at the hog . . .

➤ Look again and see what it is that makes this animal different from all others . . .

➤ Remember the things that make the hog different . . .

Have you ever seen a bat flying around in early evening? Bats are very unusual . . .

➤ Make a bat stop flying and see it in your viewer . . .

➤ Look to see how this creature is different from all others . . .

➤ Do you have it? . . .

➤ Remember it . . .

Now it is time to turn on the magic. When you turn on the magic, your viewer can show you a picture of things that do not exist . . .

➤ Let's try it by starting with a dog and a cat . . .

➤ Remember the things that made these animals different from all others? . . .

➤ Taking these things, you are going to put them on one animal . . .

➤ Look now, and see a Dogcat . . .

➤ In one picture you see an animal that looks like a dog and a cat . . .

➤ Try to remember what it looks like . . .

Going on, we'll see what other kinds of magic we might work . . .

➤ Remember the things that made a hog and a bat different? . . .

➤ You are going to use those things now . . .

➤ Turn on your viewer and see a Hogbat . . .

➤ Remember the picture of your Hogbat . . .

You have a picture of both a Dogcat and a Hogbat . . .

➤ Taking both of your pictures, combine them to make one picture . . .

➤ Look into your viewer and see a Hogdog Catbat . . .

➤ Keep looking . . .

➤ Try to see a part of each of the four animals . . .

Now I am going to give you some things about other animals that make them different from all others. Your task will be to take what I give you and try it on some other animals . . .

➤ Take the stripes of a zebra and put them on another animal . . .

➤ You should be seeing an animal with zebra stripes . . .

➤ Take the tusks of an elephant and give them to another animal . . .

➤ Take a monkey's tail and give it to another animal . . .

➤ Take the horns of a Texas steer and give them to another animal . . .

➤ When you use your imagination and your mind viewer, you can make things happen like magic.

You can create some strange new creatures . . . if you use your imagination.

Follow-Up Activities

➤ Call on players to draw pictures of any of the animals they created.

➤ Have four players make a team drawing. Each will use one of the animals in the title.

➤ In each of the above activities, have the players give a new and original name to the animal that they created.

➤ In each of the first two activities, have the players compose a story telling why this animal didn't make it to Noah's Ark.

➤ Have one player describe an animal while the second draws it.

➤ Any of the animals created may be the focus of a jingle, rhyme, or poem.

➤ Using the combination technique, have players apply it to fruit, games, automobiles, colors, and sounds.

➤ Encourage players to give elaborate descriptions and make elaborate drawings. Have them tell a complete and detailed story.

Game 15:
Mindshower

A mindshower is not quite the same as a brainstorm. When people produce a large number of ideas for solving a problem, they are brainstorming. When one or more people capture ideas in their mind and show them as images, it is called a mindshower. So, you might say that a mindshower pours ideas, and then shows them to you. Inventors, composers, and artists often use mindshowers to create new, useful, and imaginative products.

Checklisting is one of the ways you can start a mindshower. Starting with the first letter of the alphabet, I will name some things that start with the letter A. Shower pictures in your mind as I call them out . . .

➤ Apple . . .

➤ Ape . . .

➤ Angel . . .

➤ Airplane . . .

➤ Asteroid . . .

➤ Antlers . . .

➤ Armadillo . . .

➤ Automobile . . .

➤ Art . . .

Now that you have showered pictures of things starting with A, we'll go on to invent some things that you have never seen or thought of before. They will be different. Do your best to picture them in your mind. Are you ready? . . .

➤ See an antlers angel . . .

➤ See an apple asteroid . . .

➤ See an airplane arm . . .

➤ See an ape automobile . . .

➤ See an angel apple . . .

➤ See an armadillo automobile . . .

➤ See an asteroid ant . . .

➤ See an airplane automobile . . .

Now we will go to the letter B and use it to shower some things that are good to eat, see, taste, and smell. See the B things as I give them to you . . .

➤ Baked beans . . .

➤ Brown bread . . .

➤ Burgers . . .

➤ Buttered beets . . .

➤ Bacon . . .

➤ Broccoli . . .

➤ Bologna . . .

➤ Biscuits . . .

➤ Beefsteak . . .

➤ Blueberries . . .

➤ Boiled bullfrogs . . .

➤ Bubbly beverages . . .

➤ Braised bison . . .

➤ Butterscotch bagels . . .

➤ Big bananas . . .

There are many good things to eat that begin with the letter B. See, touch, smell, and taste these combinations as I give them to you . . .

➤ Butterscotch banana brown bread . . .

➤ Braised bullfrog burgers . . .

➤ Bubbly blueberry beverage . . .

➤ Bacon bits buttered broccoli . . .

➤ Boiled bologna bagels . . .

➤ Bacon baked beans on big buns . . .

➤ Did you find a combination that you really liked? . . . Remember it and be ready to tell about it.

Go on to the letter C. We'll try another kind of mindshower. I will give you the name of a business. You will see the uniform that the people in this business wear. On the front of the uniform is an emblem, patch, or design. The design will let everyone know what kind of business the person is in. Are there any questions? . . . As I give you the kinds of businesses, see the uniform and see the emblem . . .

➤ Car rental company . . .

➤ Carry-out food store . . .

➤ Clock shop . . .

➤ Computer store . . .

➤ Cat hospital . . .

➤ Cheese shop . . .

➤ Cold storage locker plant . . .

➤ Carpet cleaners . . .

➤ Clothing store . . .

With all of these designs in mind, you should be ready to create some unusual emblems. If you have a favorite, keep it in mind . . .

In playing the D game, we'll try yet another kind of mindshower. When I name something that begins with the letter D, you will try to see a picture in your mind in three dimensions. You will not only see the height and width of something, you also will see the depth. Your mind picture will be better than a colored photograph. Here we go on the 3–D photographs . . .

➤ A black and white spotted Dalmatian dog . . .

➤ A deep sea diver . . .

➤ A detective wearing a disguise . . .

➤ A deserted desert . . .

➤ A down-hearted donkey . . .

That will be all for the Ds. Remember which of the photographs you liked best. You never know what kind of great ideas you'll come up with . . . if you use your imagination.

Follow-Up Activities

Note: When using the follow-up activities, each letter game may make up a session.

➤ Ask, "Did anything unusual happen when you were playing the Mindshower Game?" Allow players to share their experiences.

➤ Following any of the given formats, call on players to write their own games using other letters of the alphabet.

➤ With reference to the C Game, have players draw any kind of emblem they wish. Other players are then given the opportunity to guess the kind of business or work represented.

➤ With any of the games, form pairs and have each person describe an image in detail, leaving nothing to the imagination of the listener.

Game 16:

Leap Before You Look

Looking before leaping is usually a good thing to do. By taking a look first, you are able to avoid problems that could turn out to be serious. When you pretend, and use your imagination, you don't have to worry about getting your bones broken, or your head split open. It is safe to take a risk and leap before you look. In playing this make-believe game, you will take giant leaps in your imagination and land in many strange and wonderful places.

I will give you the command to leap. When I say, "leap," blast off like a silver rocket streaking orange fire and billowing steamy white clouds. As you zoom through space, I will tell you where you are about to land. After a soft landing, you will have time to visit and see the sights. When it is time to end your visit, I will give you the command, "return to home base." Are there any questions? . . . Now, please listen to the instructions as you prepare to take a giant leap into space.

Ready? . . . Leave the Earth behind you and **leap** *high into space . . .*

➤ Notice that your body feels lighter as you go higher and higher . . .

➤ The Earth becomes smaller as you float upward . . .

➤ Now you are approaching Galactic I, the first city in space . . .

➤ The gate opens, and you walk into the sparkling clean city . . .

➤ The people you meet are friendly and anxious to talk to you . . .

➤ Ask them why everyone is wearing a brightly colored uniform . . .

➤ Take a last look around as you prepare to **return to home base** . . .

➤ Say goodbye to your new friends, then float back to Earth . . .

➤ Touch down at home base . . .

Get ready to take another leap . . .

➤ Are you ready? . . .

➤ **Leap** high into the air . . .

➤ Now, slowly tumble back to Earth . . .

➤ You have landed on a raft and are floating down a river . . .

➤ Get comfortable, then view all there is to view as you float along . . .

➤ From downstream, a boat moves closer to you . . .

➤ Wave back to the people who are waving to you . . .

➤ Over to your right, you can see a town in the distance . . .

➤ As you get closer, the buildings get larger . . .

➤ You decide to stop at the town and look for a place to land . . .

➤ Stretch, look around, and get ready to **return to home base** . . .

➤ Touch down at home base . . .

Get ready to leap . . .

➤ **Leap** . . .

➤ You are landing in a country far, far away . . .

➤ You are in a strange city, and strange people are all around you . . .

➤ Walk down the street and look into the store windows . . .

➤ Stop at a restaurant and order your lunch . . .

➤ Thank your waitress and taste your lunch . . .

➤ Do you like it? . . .

➤ If you do, finish your lunch and pay for it . . .

➤ Walk out of the restaurant and **return to home base** . . .

➤ Touch down . . .

It is leap time again. Get ready to leap. . . .

➤ **Leap** . . .

➤ You come down through billowy dark clouds and the day is wet and windy . . .

➤ You find yourself alone in a dimly lit hallway of a deserted castle . . .

➤ Mist is rolling down the hallway toward you . . .

➤ As you look and listen, you hear strange sounds . . .

➤ As the mist comes closer . . .

➤ You see a ghost in front of you . . .

➤ Talk to the ghost. Try to find out something about it . . .

➤ Now a dazzling bright light appears down the hallway . . .

➤ It gets brighter and brighter . . .

➤ It is time to leave the castle and **return to home base** . . .

➤ Touch down at home base . . .

It's easy to be brave and daring . . . when you use your imagination.

Follow-Up Activities

➤ Call on players to share the senses experienced in each of the games: Sound, taste, touch, sight, and odor.

➤ Call on players to picture a life-like experience in any of the games and describe it in detail.

➤ Call on players to make a drawing of the most vivid vision that they experienced in any of the games.

➤ Two or more players may be used to write a scenario, and then act it out.

➤ The leader may take players on a blind leap without a designated place to land. Players are then free to land any place they wish. The experiences of the blind leap may be used to write a short story.

Game 17:

Oops!

The word "oops" is used to express surprise. When things take a turn away from the expected, we may respond by saying, "Oops!" In the game that you are about to play, *Oops!* will be used as a watchword that tells you to complete a rhyme on your own. You will picture the rhyme in your imagination and then go on to invent an unexpected ending. There will be no wrong answers. See an ending that will be unusual, clever, and one of a kind. Close your eyes and be ready to see the rhyme and give it an ending.

➤ Little Polly Flanders . . .
  Sat among the cinders . . .
  Oops! . . .

➤ Dickory, dickory dare . . .
  The pig flew up in the air . . .
  Oops! . . .

➤ Jack and Jill went up the hill . . .
  To fetch a pail of water . . .

Jack fell down . . .
Oops! . . .

➤ Old Mother Twitchett had but one eye . . .
And a long tail which she let fly . . .
And every time she went through a gap . . .
Oops! . . .

➤ Wee Willie Winkie runs through the town . . .
Upstairs and downstairs in his nightgown . . .
Oops! . . .

➤ There was a man in our town . . .
And he was wondrous wise . . .
He jumped into a bramble bush . . .
Oops! . . .

➤ Little Miss Muffet . . .
Sat on a Tuffet . . .
Eating her curds and whey . . .
There came a big spider . . .
and Oops! . . .

➤ Humpty Dumpty sat on a wall . . .
Humpty Dumpty had a great fall . . .
Oops! . . .

➤ Old Mother Hubbard . . .
Went to the cupboard . . .
To get her poor dog a bone . . .
But when she got there . . .
Oops! . . .

➤ There were once two cats of Kilkenny . . .
Each thought there was one cat too many . . .
Oops! . . .

➤ Hey diddle, diddle! . . .
The cat and the fiddle . . .
The cow jumped over the moon . . .
Oops! . . .

➤ I saw a ship a-sailing . . .
A-sailing on the sea . . .
And, Oh! It was all laden . . .
With pretty things for thee . . .
Oops! . . .

➤ There was a fat man of Bombay . . .
Smoking his pipe one sunshiny day . . .
When a bird called a snipe. . .
Oops! . . .

It's easy and breezy to rhyme in time . . . when you use your imagination.

Follow-Up Activity

➤ Taking the rhymes one at a time, call on players to write their own original endings. Players also may be called on to compose their own rhymes making provision for an Oops! ending.

Game 18:

Room for the Future

Using your imagination, you are able to make plans and see things ahead of time. When you direct your mind to think and create images, you are able to design the future just the way you want it to be. In the game we are about to play, you will be using your mind to plan, see, and design the future. You will plan your own room, then you will picture it in your mind.

To do this, you will design parts of the room one at a time. Then, you will take the parts and join them together as you plan your room for the future. Work hard to see good pictures in your mind. The harder you try, the clearer the pictures will be. Are you ready to create a design for the future? All right then, let's start.

First, you will need a window. You may make it any size, shape, or style that you wish to make it. See a picture in your mind of the window that you want . . .

➤ Now that you have a window, you have something to look out of . . .

➤ When you look out of your window, you'll be able to see whatever you wish to see. What do you wish to see? . . .

➤ Look out of your window and see those things . . .

Next, you will need to have a door. Doors come in many shapes, sizes, colors, and designs. Think about the kind of door you wish to have . . .

➤ Take a good look at the door that you have selected . . .

➤ Now that you have a door, you will need to make some decisions about it . . .

➤ If you open the door, it will lead to someplace . . .

➤ There is something on the other side of the door . . .

➤ What do you want it to be? . . .

➤ Now open the door and see those things . . .

➤ Take a good look . . .

➤ Shut the door . . .

You have a window and a door. You need some walls to put them in . . .

➤ Your walls may be any color you want them to be . . .

➤ If you wish, you may select colorful wallpaper . . .

➤ See your walls the way you want them to be . . .

➤ Do you want pictures or anything else on your walls? . . .

➤ Place those things on your walls . . .

It is time to start building your room for the future . . .

➤ Take your window and place it in one of the walls . . .

➤ Stand back and take a look at it . . .

➤ Take your door and put it in another wall . . .

➤ Take a good look at your wall and door . . .

➤ Do you like what you see? . . .

➤ Make whatever changes you wish to make . . .

Before your room for the future is completed, there is something more to be added. You will need a floor . . .

➤ How do you wish the floor to appear? . . .

➤ Think of ways it might appear . . .

➤ Decide how you wish your floor to appear, then picture it just the way you want it to be . . .

➤ Walk across the floor . . .

➤ See a picture of your windows, walls, and door . . .

➤ Make any changes you wish to make . . .

You now have your room for the future, but it is empty . . .

➤ Before selecting furnishings for the room, you will need to decide how it is to be used . . .

➤ What are the many kinds of rooms that it might be? . . .

➤ Think about this . . .

➤ Decide what kind of room it will be . . .

➤ How will it be used? . . .

➤ It is time to go shopping for the things that you will use to furnish your room . . .

➤ Take the furnishings you have selected and arrange them in the room the way you want them to be . . .

➤ Do you like the arrangement? . . .

➤ If you wish to make any changes, go ahead and make them . . .

Listen, someone is knocking on the door . . .

➤ Who might be coming to visit you? . . .

➤ Open the door and invite him or her in . . .

➤ Show the visitor your room for the future and tell him or her how it is to be used . . .

➤ It is time for your visitor to leave . . .

➤ Show him or her to the door and tell the visitor goodbye . . .

➤ Now shut the door and turn out the lights . . .

You can design the house of your dreams . . . if you use your imagination.

Follow-Up Activities

➤ Call on players to give verbal descriptions of their rooms, or parts of their rooms. Call for elaborate, detailed descriptions.

➤ Determine the different kinds of rooms that were selected. Ask players why their rooms will be particularly useful in the future.

➤ Role-play the visitor knocking at the door. The selected player will show the visitor about the room describing how the room is to be used.

➤ Call on players to give their room a name. The name may suggest the future and hint at how the room will be used.

Game 19:

Handy Randy, the Space-Age Robot

Some people think that the inventor is a strange person. Others believe that he is a genius, and mention the fact that he holds more than 100 patents. Walking to and from his laboratory, he often stops to talk to you. You have found the inventor to be both interesting and friendly. One evening the inventor stops to talk and invites you to visit his laboratory to meet Handy Randy, the space-age robot.

The next morning you meet the inventor, and together you walk to the laboratory. On the way, he tells you that he has succeeded in using alpha waves to computerize the robot's brain. If you know the secret, the robot can be programmed to do anything that people do. It also can float in the air and become invisible.

As you enter the laboratory, you promise that you will keep all secrets that are given to you. The inventor then tells you that when your brain waves are tuned to the robot's signal, the robot will respond to the commands that are given. The inventor also tells you that the robot will become invisible when you send one silent beep. Send two silent beeps and it becomes visible again. You have learned to control the robot.

Now you are ready to meet Handy Randy...

➤ You are excited...

➤ Your heart beats faster...

➤ The eventful moment has arrived. You are about to meet Handy Randy, the space-age robot...

➤ Pointing, the inventor tells you that the robot is behind the blue curtain . . .

➤ As he pulls the cord and opens the curtain, there stands Randy . . .

➤ Take a good look at him . . .

➤ Tune your brain waves to the robot's signal . . .

➤ The robot is now at your command. Send the message, "Take three steps forward." . . .

➤ Send one silent beep . . .

➤ Send two silent beeps . . .

➤ Command the robot to take three steps backward . . .

➤ Turn off the signal . . .

Your new friend tells you that you have done quite well in learning how to command the robot . . .

➤ He then tells you to listen for further instructions . . .

➤ First, whatever you say silently to yourself when you are on the robot's signal, the robot will repeat using your voice . . .

➤ The inventor then tells you that you will be given command of the robot for one week if you promise to make a complete report . . .

➤ You promise to make the report . . .

Now it will be your task to take the robot out of the laboratory and to your home . . .

Think about it . . .

➤ How are you going to do this? . . .

➤ Using your imagination, see yourself taking the robot home with you . . .

➤ Now it is time to write a computerized program for Randy . . .

➤ Program the robot to sit at the table when you are eating your evening meal . . .

➤ Remember, Randy can be visible or invisible . . .

➤ He can talk using your voice, pass food around the table, and go to the kitchen to bring in anything you might want . . .

➤ In your mind, write the Evening Meal Program for the robot . . .

Now it is time to eat and Randy is sitting at the table with you . . .

➤ Using your imagination, watch to see what happens . . .

➤ Having completed your meal, you will need to write a Tomorrow Program for the robot's computer . . .

➤ Where will you go? . . .

➤ Who will you see? . . .

➤ What will you do? . . .

➤ Include the robot in your plans as you write the program in your mind . . .

➤ It is now tomorrow . . .

➤ Make brain wave contact with the robot and watch to see what happens . . .

Handy Randy is like a mechanical twin. Like your shadow, the robot trails along with you wherever you go . . .

➤ Think of some places that you would like to take Handy Randy . . .

➤ Maybe a ball game, the zoo, a party, or to the supermarket . . .

➤ Think about the places you would like to take the robot . . .

➤ Choose one of them and write a program in your mind . . .

➤ Now command the robot to perform the program that you have written . . .

➤ Remember, Randy can be visible or invisible . . .

➤ Watch to see how well he performs . . .

The week is now over. You must return the robot to the laboratory. As you knock on the door, think of the report that you will make to the inventor . . .

Your robot friend can do some amazing things . . . if you use your imagination.

Follow-Up Activities

➤ Have the players draw a picture of the robot as they saw it.

➤ Have players give, or write, a report as they would give it to the inventor.

➤ Have players write a short story on the topics: The Day My Robot Left Home Without Me or The Day I Stayed Home and Sent the Robot.

➤ Also consider a robot play or robot model as a follow-up.

2070 Script Writer

A script is an author's copy of a play, novel, movie, broadcast, or telecast. For every story that you read, and every program that you watch, someone has written the story that goes along with the action. Operating behind the scenes, the scriptwriters are the people who create the stories. Using their imagination, they produce clever, interesting, original stories, plays, and programs. You can be a scriptwriter for events to take place in the year 2070, if you use your imagination. To do this, you will need to project your thinking far into the future, and roam around in your mind for far out ideas and images.

The script that you are about to write will be in four parts. You will think about, and see, the story parts one at a time. After seeing all four parts, you will then go back and join the parts together to form a complete story. If the story parts don't seem to fit as you go along, don't worry about it. If you are ready, turn on your image-making machine and we'll go to Part I.

Your script for the year 2070 will have to be about someone or something. Your main character may be a person, animal, or a thing . . .

➤ In your mind, make a list of the main characters that you wish to consider . . .

➤ Now choose the character that you wish to appear in your script, and see that character in great detail . . .

➤ Place the picture of your main character in the corner of your mind as we go on to Part II of your story . . .

Where do you want your story to take place? It could take place anywhere on Earth, at sea, or in space . . .

➤ Let your mind drift far and wide as you think about the many places that your story could happen . . .

➤ Now choose one of those places . . .

➤ Think about the places you would like to take the robot . . .

➤ We'll call it the setting . . .

➤ See the setting in great detail . . .

➤ See it as if you were really there . . .

➤ See all there is to see about it . . .

➤ Now place the picture of the setting in another corner of your mind as we go on to Part III of your story . . .

In the third part of your story, you'll be searching for things that might happen. Of course, in your imagination, anything could happen . . .

➤ We will call these things events or incidents. An incident is something that could have a serious outcome . . .

➤ It helps to shape the turn of events. Some examples are: finding a lost wallet, being mistaken for a robber, being lost in space, or having the law of gravity repealed . . .

➤ In your mind, run through some images of unusual incidents that might take place . . .

➤ Choose one incident that you believe will be different from anything that anyone else will think of . . .

➤ Got it? See it . . .

➤ Run it through and watch it take place . . .

➤ You will come back to the incident later. Right now put it aside as we go on to Part IV of your story . . .

Sooner or later, all things come to an end. A story ending tells us how things turned out. Some examples of endings are: the big game was won or lost; the lost treasure was found; a safe rescue was made; and the laser beam finally reached the moon . . .

➤ Turning on your magic viewer, see some unusual ways in which your story might end . . .

➤ Don't worry about the rest of the story, just see some endings . . .

➤ A good ending provides a surprise. Select a surprise ending, then run it through in sound and color in your imagination . . .

You have now written a story script for the year 2070. As I call out the parts, see them once again . . .

➤ Main character . . .

➤ The setting . . .

➤ The incident that took place . . .

➤ And last, the story ending . . .

➤ Your task now will be to take the parts of the story and weave them together to form a complete script . . .

➤ If the parts don't fit together, then you will need to find some ways to make them connect . . .

➤ You can do that by using your imagination . . .

➤ Take the parts of the story and see it all happen, like a movie in your head . . .

➤ Remember your script, and be ready to tell or write about it . . .

You can travel as far into the future as you would like . . . if you use your imagination.

Follow-Up Activities

➤ Call on players to tell or write about their script.

➤ Have the players use their script to write a play.

➤ Call on players to describe a part of their script; the first player describes the character, the second player describes the setting, and so on.

➤ Call on four players to rewrite the script using the data from all four-story scripts.

Appendix A:
SCAMPER on Your Own

As written, the SCAMPER games present a detailed step-by-step guide for developing creative imagination. For the most part, players are asked to visualize and form mental images from the cues that are given. The major emphasis of the games is placed on nonverbal expression. This has been done with a purpose in mind. It was the intent of the author to present a simple and clear format that would be easily adaptable to particular groups and situations.

The opportunities for verbal or written expression are unlimited. Game leaders are encouraged to SCAMPER on their own and to make adaptations to suit their own style and game situations. As leaders gain self-assurance through familiarity with the games, it is hoped that they will create their own original ways of playing. The thinking and feeling processes and the SCAMPER techniques presented earlier are suggestive of new and original ways to SCAMPER.

Optional Activities for Getting Started on Your Own

➤ In playing or replaying the games, instruct players to act out the directions or cues given. Remember, dramatic activity will require movement on the part of the players as they role-play their imaginative experiences. It will be necessary for the leader to determine the rules that will be used and to pass his or her expectations on to the players.

➤ For example, the leader may wish to make the following rules, "No one is to take more than two steps in any direction." "Do not make movements that will cause you to touch another player." "You are to act out the directions without speaking." Playing background music that is familiar to the players may enhance the dramatic activity.

➤ Play the games as presented in the script with one exception. With this option, players are asked, at certain times, to answer selected cues verbally. The leader will need to read through the script and preselect the cues that will be used for this purpose. A checkmark may be placed in the book to identify the cue that is to be used for verbal response. When more than one person is playing, it is suggested that all be given an opportunity to respond. In view of the fact that more time will be consumed in using this option, it would be a good idea to establish time limits before starting the game.

➤ This option provides for written response. Each player or team of players should have paper and pencil available before starting. Once again, the leader will need to preselect the cues to be used. A review of the thinking and feeling processes presented earlier will be of help in identifying the categories of thought singled out for development.

➤ Play the game, or part of a game, stopping to provide time for players to record their thoughts. For example, in the Cardboard Box game, you might cue players to make a list of the different kinds of vegetables that they could put in a refrigerator. In the New Zoo game, the players may be asked to record the names they have given to the animals. In the Doughnuts game, players may be asked to write a list of all of the good things to eat that they could put inside of a doughnut. In What in the World Did You Find?, players could make a record of their observations. Time may be taken to allow players to discuss the ideas and observations that they have recorded.

Appendix B:
SCAMPER With Adults

These games have been successfully used with college students enrolled in creative studies courses, and with other adults in training sessions. The SCAMPER techniques have been widely published and applied in the creation of new products. When used with adults, the games have proven to be of value in several ways:

> ➤ gaining involvement of individuals in the group,

> ➤ arousing curiosity and setting levels of expectation,

> ➤ warming up individuals to creative thinking tasks,

> ➤ teaching and practicing the SCAMPER techniques,

> ➤ building and enhancing mental images, and

> ➤ applying processes often associated with creative expression.

In gaining these outcomes, adults should be assured that they are not playing fun and games. It may be fun, but it is not simply *for* fun! Use of imagery and mental manipulative skills are the common tools of inventors, designers, composers, and artists. The games have proven to be a great leveling activity. All may play. All may contribute ideas and share experiences. All may win; there are no wrong answers. And, as volunteered by a sixth grader, "It's fair for all, and nobody can cheat."

Before introducing the games to adults, it is recommended that time be taken to explain the SCAMPER Checklist. The general nature of the checklist, and its use in gaining problem-solving ideas, should be explained. Make it clear that the idea-spurring techniques are woven into the games, and that they may be enhanced by playing. Trying improves imagery; it also improves creative expression. Approach adults with the same enthusiasm that you would display with children.

New Zoo (Adult Version)

Let's take a few minutes to play a game called SCAMPER. It is a game for imagination and development. The book, *SCAMPER*, is actually designed for use with children. We are going to play an adult version of one of the games.

First, let me ask you to think back to when you were 9 years old . . .

➤ Do you remember the name of the school that you attended? . . .

➤ There were some things you did very well as a third grader. One of them was skipping . . .

➤ When was the last time you skipped? . . . (You may ask if anyone would like to skip around the room.)

➤ There was another thing you did very well as a third grader. You used your imagination . . .

➤ Using your imagination is what the SCAMPER games are all about, and that is what I am going to ask you to do.

It is very important for you to concentrate in order to imagine . . .

➤ So, please close your eyes . . .

➤ Forget about the person sitting next to you . . .

➤ Forget about the room you are in . . .

➤ Forget about the tables, chairs, and other things in the room . . .

➤ Concentrate on my voice and what I tell you to do . . .

A moose has a big head and antlers . . .

➤ Can you visualize this? . . . Can you see the antlers? . . .

➤ Take his big head and put it on a hippopotamus . . .

➤ Look at this animal very carefully . . .

➤ Observe his unique characteristics . . .

➤ Touch him . . .

➤ Walk around him . . .

➤ Can you see him? . . .

➤ All right . . .

Now open your eyes . . .

➤ It is your task to give this animal a name. A name that will help to describe him to others . . .

➤ Close your eyes once again and create a mental picture of this animal . . .

➤ See him as before and create a mental picture of this animal . . .

➤ See him and imagine how this animal might live . . .

➤ Go to fantastic extremes and think of his habits . . .

➤ Using all of the imaginative information you have built up, search around for combinations of words that will form a new and descriptive name . . .

➤ Create a new name . . .

➤ Do you have it? . . .

➤ Good. Remember it . . .

Now open your eyes . . .

➤ Will you share the name you created with others? . . .

➤ We will take a few minutes for you to share your experiences with others and tell them the name that you gave the animal . . .

Optional New Zoo Activities

➤ Have the players draw a picture of the animal. Place the name of the animal at the bottom of the picture.

➤ Ask players to give an elaborate verbal description of the animal.

➤ Provide teams of players with pictures of animals taken from magazines. Provide scissors, paste, and background paper and have them create their own animals and name them. Give a prize for the most artistically unique production.

➤ Have players list the numbers 1 through 10 vertically on a sheet of paper. For each number, have them list an animal and name the most unique characteristic of the animal. When this task is completed, the leader randomly selects two numbers (e.g., 3 and 9) and asks the players to combine the characteristics and name the animals.

➤ Have players write the word SCAMPER vertically on their paper. Supply the appropriate words for each letter of SCAMPER and comment on the intellectual processes involved in SCAMPERing.

➤ Using Appendix A: SCAMPER on Your Own, develop other ideas that you may wish to adapt for use with adults.

Creative Imagination Development

Knowing and understanding the thinking and feeling processes associated with creative expression makes it possible to single out those abilities and focus on their development. Borrowing from the work of Frank E. Williams, the cognitive and affective processes associated with creativity are placed in an interactive mode and illustrated in the SCAMPER model. The mental manipulations represented by the SCAMPER techniques are then added to the model and used as a vehicle for process development. In combination, the cognitive and affective processes, plus the idea-spurring techniques, provide the foundation and framework upon which the SCAMPER games were built.

Cognitive Processes Contributing to Creative Expression

Fluent Thinking

➤ The free flow of thought.

➤ The generation of quantity, the most.

➤ A large number of relevant responses.

Flexible Thinking

➤ Providing for shifts in categories of thought.

➤ Entertaining differing points of view.

➤ Considering alternate plans.

Originality

➤ The production of unusual or unanticipated responses.

➤ Characterized by novelty and uniqueness.

➤ Considering alternate plans.

Elaboration

➤ To refine, embellish, or enrich an idea, plan, or product.

➤ To make a simple idea or response elegant by adding detail.

➤ To provide illuminating, descriptive dimensions.

Affective Processes Contributing to Creative Expression

Curiosity

➤ A strong desire to know about something.

➤ To wonder about, to be inquisitive.

➤ Having the capacity to be puzzled.

Willingness to Take Calculated Risks

➤ Freedom to take a guess, not fearful of being wrong.

➤ Speculation, prediction, and foresight are involved.

➤ Liking the unknown, adventurous.

Preference for Complexity

➤ Likes to bring order out of chaos.

➤ Desires to work with details and knotty problems.

➤ Willingly accepts a challenge.

Intuition

➤ Quick and keen insight.

➤ Plays hunches.

➤ Perceives ideas or information independent of reasoning processes.

Right Hemisphere Specialization

Traditionally, education has placed a heavy emphasis on brain functions attributed to the left hemisphere. Creative expression places an emphasis on brain functions attributed to the right hemisphere. Highly creative individuals prefer distinct ways of learning and interacting, as described below.

A highly creative individual:

➤ prefers visual explanations,

➤ processes information holistically,

➤ prefers abstract thinking tasks,

➤ expresses emotions openly,

➤ prefers to gain general overview,

➤ uses images to remember,

➤ produces ideas intuitively,

➤ deals with many tasks at once,

➤ approaches problems playfully, and

➤ likes open, fluid experiences.

Appendix D:
SCAMPER Model for Creative Imagination Development

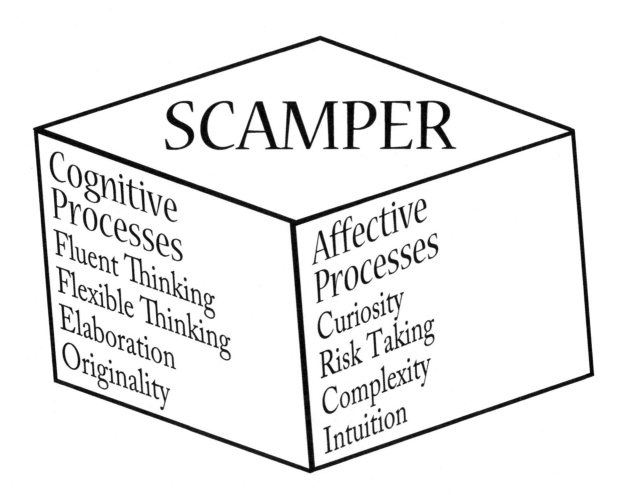

Note. From Williams, F. E., (1970). *Classroom ideas for encouraging thinking and feeling.* Buffalo, NY: D.O.K.

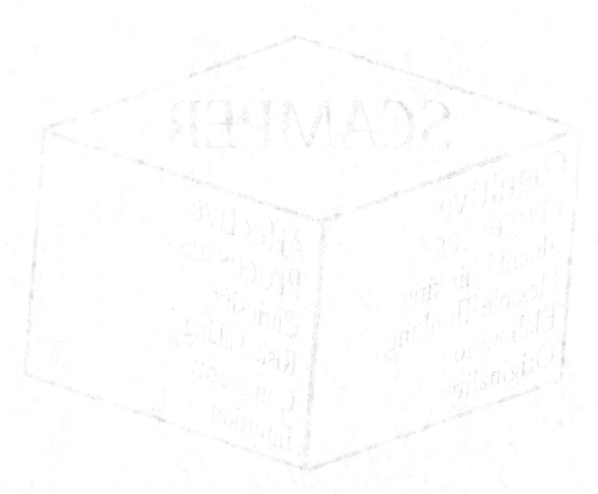

Resources for Imagery and Creativity

Arnheim, R. (2004). *Visual thinking.* Los Angeles: The University of California Press.

Biondi, A. M. (Ed.). (1974). *Have an affair with your mind.* Great Neck, NY: Creative Synergetic Associates.

DeBono, E. E. (1973). *Lateral thinking: Creativity step by step.* New York: Harper Collins.

Eberle, B. (1982). *Chip in: Motivational activities to stimulate better thinking.* Carthage, IL: Good Apple.

Eberle, B. (1983). *Apple shines: Polishing student writing skills.* Carthage, IL: Good Apple.

Eberle, B. (1984). *Help! in solving problems creatively at home and school.* Carthage, IL: Good Apple.

Eberle, B., & Stanish, B. (1996). *CPS for kids: A resource book for teaching creative problem-solving to children.* Waco, TX: Prufrock Press.

Edwards, B. (1989). *Drawing on the right side of the brain.* Los Angeles: J. P. Tarcher.

Elwell, P. A., & Treffinger, D. J. (Eds.). (1993). *CPS for teens: Classroom activities for teaching creative problem solving.* Waco, TX: Prufrock Press.

Gorden, W. J. J. (1961). *Synectics: The development of creative capacity.* New York: Harper Collins.

Gowan, J. C. (1972). *Development of the creative individual.* San Diego, CA: Knapp.

Gowan, J. C. (1975). *Trance, art, and creativity.* Buffalo, NY: The Creative Education Foundation.

Guilford, J. P. (1967). *The nature of human intelligence*. New York: McGraw-Hill.

Guilford, J. P. (1977). *Way beyond the I.Q.* Buffalo, NY: The Creative Education Foundation.

Mackinnon, D. W. (1978). *In search of human effectiveness: Identifying and developing creativity*. Buffalo, NY: The Creative Education Foundation.

McIntosh, J. E., & Meacham, A. W. (1991). *Creative problem solving in the classroom: A teacher's guide to using CPS effectively in any classroom*. Waco, TX: Prufrock Press.

Noller, R. B., Treffinger, D. J., & Houseman, E. D. (1979). *It's a gas to be gifted: Or CPS for the gifted and talented*. Buffalo, NY: D.O.K.

Noller, R. B. (1977). *Scratching the surface of creative problem solving: A bird's eye view of CPS*. Buffalo, NY: D.O.K.

Ornstein, R. (1996). *The psychology of consciousness* (2nd ed.). New York: Penguin.

Osborn, A. F. (1979). *Applied imagination: Principles and procedures of creative problem solving*. New York: Charles Scribner's Sons.

Parnes, S. J. (1981). *The magic of your mind*. Buffalo, NY: The Creative Education Foundation.

Rugg, H. (1963). *Imagination: An inquiry into the sources and conditions that stimulate creativity*. New York: Harper & Row.

Samuels, M., & Samuels, N. (1975). *Seeing with the mind's eye: The history, techniques, and uses of visualization*. New York: Random House.

Shallcross, D. J. (1980). *Teaching creative behavior: How to teach creativity to children of all ages*. Englewood Cliffs, NJ: Prentice-Hall.

Stanish, B., & Eberle, B. (1997). *Be a problem solver: A resource book for teaching creative problem solving*. Waco, TX: Prufrock Press.

Torrance, E. P. (1979). *The search for Satori and creativity*. Buffalo, NY: The Creative Education Foundation.

Williams, F. E. (1971). *Classroom ideas for encouraging thinking and feeling*. Buffalo, NY: D.O.K.

Printed in the United States
by Baker & Taylor Publisher Services